Brilliant Publications

Fun with Poems

Brilliant Publications

Contents

Introduction 4
Response 5
Understanding Form, Style, Theme and Subject Matter 5
Literacy Hour 7
Encouraging Children's Own Writing 8
Notes on Poems 10
Poems 22
Indexes 102

Contents of Poems and their place in the NLS programme

Title	page	Year 3			Year 4			Year 5			Year 6		
	no.	T1	T2	T3	T1	T2	T3	T1	T2	T3	T1	T2	T3
Best Friend	22	*			*			*				*	*
Poetry Jump-up	23	*	*	*	*	*	*	*		*		*	*
Voices in my Head	24	*	*	*				*		*		*	*
Timothy	25	*		*			*	*				*	*
My Eyes Are Watering	26	*			*			*					*
Shame	27	*			*			*					
No Ordinary Day	28	*			*		*	*				*	*
Safe Crossing	29	*			*			*					*
What Next?	30	*					*	*				*	*
Days	31	*			*			*					*
Hiawatha's Childhood	32	*	*			*	*	*	*	*	*	*	*
Holiday in Colour	34	*		*	*		*	*				*	*
My Street Is Different ..	35	*	*				*	*		*			*
Eldorado	36	*	*			*			*	*	*		
Stormy Temper	37	*			*			*		*			*
From a Railway Carriage	38	*	*	*	*	*	*	*		*	*	*	*
Big Fears	39	*			*			*					*
Sun Candle	40	*	*					*		*		*	*
A Cook's Tour of ...	41	*		*	*		*	*				*	
Alien Nightmare	42	*		*	*			*					*
Market Razzle-Dazzle	43	*	*	*			*	*		*			*
Stadium Wood	44	*	*	*				*					*
In the Swim	45	*	*	*	*		*	*		*			*
Left Back	46	*		*	*			*					*
My Dad Is Very Keen ...	47	*		*	*			*					*
Red Card	48	*		*	*		*	*					*
Ten Things to Do with ...	49	*		*	*		*	*				*	*
Space Probe	50	*		*	*			*		*			*
Blast-off!	51	*	*	*	*			*					*
Seeing St*rs	52	*		*	*		*	*				*	*
Our Holiday on the Moon	53	*		*	*			*		*			*

Title	page	Year 3			Year 4			Year 5			Year 6		
	no.	T1	T2	T3	T1	T2	T3	T1	T2	T3	T1	T2	T3
Escape at Bedtime	54	*			*	*	*	*			*	*	*
Maybe There's a New ...	55	*		*	*			*		*			*
In Our Family	56	*		*	*			*					*
My Little Sister	57	*		*	*		*	*					*
My Gran	58	*		*	*		*	*					*
Oh Gran!	59	*		*	*			*					*
Granny Is a Sprinter	60	*		*	*			*					*
Grandpa	61	*			*			*					*
Mum's Infallible Method ...	62	*		*	*			*					*
Feeling Peckish	63	*		*	*			*					*
True Confession	64	*			*			*					*
Children Menu	65	*		*			*	*					*
A–Z of People and ...	66	*		*	*		*	*					*
Ice Cream	67	*		*	*			*					*
Did You See?	68	*			*			*		*			
Windy Nights	69	*				*	*	*			*		*
A Rhyme	70	*		*	*	*							
Five Answers to the...	71	*			*		*	*		*			*
Winter	72	*	*		*	*	*			*	*	*	*
Christmas Shopping ...	73	*			*		*	*					*
Rubrik for Enjoying ...	74	*			*		*	*		*			*
Shopping List for ...	75	*		*	*		*	*				*	*
Bonfire Party	76	*			*		*	*		*		*	*
Low Owl	77	*			*		*	*		*		*	*
Polar Bear	78	*	*		*		*	*		*		*	*
The Eagle	79	*			*	*	*			*	*	*	
The Aquarium	80	*		*	*			*					*
Skunks	81	*		*	*			*					*
Dragons' Wood	82	*			*		*	*		*			*
Midnight Badgers	83	*			*			*		*			*
Akol and the Giraffe	84	*	*		*	*	*	*	*	*		*	*
How the Tortoise Got...	86	*			*	*	*	*		*			*
Hurt No Living Thing	88	*			*	*	*	*		*	*	*	*
Insect	89	*		*	*		*	*					*
Advice about Dogs	90	*		*	*		*	*					*
Jabberwocky	91	*		*	*	*	*	*	*	*	*	*	*
Death	92	*			*		*	*					*
Births/Marriages/Deaths	93	*		*	*		*	*					*
Lambs	94	*			*			*					*
Nick's Cat	95	*					*	*					*
Seagulls in the City	96	*			*		*	*		*		*	*
Up in the Air	98	*			*		*	*		*		*	*
One Wicked Weasel	99	*	*		*		*	*		*		*	*
How Doth the Little...	100	*		*	*	*		*		*	*	*	*
The Silent Snake	101	*			*	*							

Introduction

Poetry stirs the soul and stimulates the mind with words and sounds to bring pleasure. A love of poetry is a great gift because it enriches our lives by making sense of the most incredible events, hopes, dreams and feelings. It inspires a fascination for words – words which take us from tears to laughter, from grief to joy, from misapprehension to understanding.

Teaching poetry is about developing enjoyment and response: it is about stimulating pupils towards considered response and towards thinking about how words may be put together to create effect; it is about leading pupils to write poems that have a clear message and meaning for others.

Response

All responses to poems are valid. Our responses are conditioned by our own feelings, experiences, likes and dislikes. We may love a poem's rhyme and rhythm, or be inspired not by its form but by its expression of ideas, its irony, its use of metaphor, its sound – or simply by the feel of the words playing on the tongue.

What we want our pupils to do, and it is a struggle to begin with, is to find out exactly *why* they like or dislike a poem. What is it that excites them or turns them off? What is it that inspires them or makes them bored? What is it that appeals or has nothing to say?

Understanding Form, Style, Theme and Subject matter

Teach them about *form, style, theme and subject matter* – how these four elements go together to make a poem and how they differ.

Form

Form is pattern. *Haiku, sonnet, cinquain, limerick and ballad* are well-known forms. There are many others. Poems do not have to be written in known forms – form can develop as the writing progresses. It is crucial that the chosen form is appropriate to the ideas or message of the poem – a poem of grief, for example, would not be right in the form of a limerick. Writing poems in specific forms is a great challenge for children.

Style

Style is a part of a poet's personality. It is moulded by the kind of person the poet is. Often a poet's work will reflect the style of other poets, but it will never be exactly the same. The poet's style is the poet's 'voice' and is quite recognisable. Style is all about the kind of words the poet uses, the kind of imagery (metaphor and simile), the things that mark the poem out as having been written by a specific poet.

Theme

Theme is really 'What is the poem trying to tell us?' Sometimes the poem may be light-hearted and bubbly and not really seem to have much of a theme at all, but there will always be an underlying truth in its message, no matter how simple the poem may appear to be. That underlying truth is its theme.

Subject matter

Subject matter is what the poem is, overtly, all about. Again, the theme and the subject matter must match the form and the writer's style. If any of them don't go happily together, then the poem will not 'gel'.

Prod gently to get the children to work out what it is they 'like' or 'don't like' about a poem. Don't labour the point of 'understanding'. Poems can be enjoyed without any understanding whatsoever – the sounds, the feel of the syllables on the tongue, the rhymes, the alliteration, the onomatopoeia – all of these combine to make a poem pleasurable.

This book of poems has been specially written for children aged between 7 and 11 (with the exception of the traditional poems), to fit in with the National Literacy Strategy. Its companion book is Fun With Plays and within the two you will find much of the material you need for your NLS lessons. All of the poems can be photocopied or enlarged. We have used large typefaces so that they can be used directly on to an OHP. Notes for each poem follow this section.

Literacy Hour

Please note that no-one associated with this book would suggest for one moment that any of the poems can be used only during a certain term or at a certain time. We have shown which terms they fit into most easily, within the ranges of the NLS, but that is not because we think they should be used ONLY at those times, it is merely as a helpful indicator for the teacher.

How the poem themes fit into the NLS spectrum

Year 3/ Term 1 – Poems based on observation and senses, shape poems.

Year 3/ Term 2 – Oral and performance poetry from different cultures.

Year 3/ Term 3 – Humorous poetry, poetry that plays with language, word puzzles, puns, riddles.

Year 4/ Term 1 – Common themes – for example: school, animals, families, feelings, viewpoints, etc.

Year 4/ Term 2 – Classic and modern poetry, including poems from different cultures and times.

Year 4/ Term 3 – Range of poetry in different forms – poems that have interesting and unusual forms to examine with the children – see each poem's individual notes for more information about its form.

Year 5/ Term 1 – Poems by significant children's writers, concrete poetry. All the poets in this book (other than the traditional ones) are writing and contributing regularly to contemporary anthologies of all kinds, and therefore can be considered to be 'significant poets'.

Year 5/ Term 2 – Longer classic poetry including narrative poetry.

Year 5/ Term 3 – Poems from a variety of cultures and traditions, choral and performance poetry.

Year 6/ Term 1 – Classic poetry by long-established poets.

Year 6/ Term 2 – Range of poetic forms.

Year 6/ Term 3 – Work by same poet for comparison and work based on same theme for comparison.

Encouraging Children's Own Writing

Stress that a poem has to make *sense* – even a nonsense rhyme has to have some underlying logic to it. Having to make sense of their words will take away the children's urge for their poems to rhyme at all costs – often if they begin a complicated rhyming pattern they will use any old word because it rhymes, regardless of the nonsense it creates.

A poem can't be wrong – if it is their poem, in their voice, and it gives the message they want to imply, then it is right. Once it is right, they need to think about whether it is good. Can they improve on their vocabulary or inject some alliteration, onomatopoeia, metaphor, simile? Can they improve it by changing the punctuation?

Provide a thesaurus and expect them to use it – a poet chooses words with accuracy – there are millions of words in the ether, but the poet has to capture exactly the right ones to be happy with the poem. Good tools, also, are a spelling dictionary, a rhyming dictionary, a dictionary of appropriate adjectives, a book of idioms, a dictionary of synonyms and antonyms, a book of phrases and proverbs – all of these will help to sharpen the children's vocabulary once they get used to using them.

Try writing class or group poems to start with. Brainstorm a topic and perhaps a form and ask for someone to come up with a good opening line. Encourage constructive criticism – 'Perhaps it would sound better if. . .' – and get everyone to join in.

Use the poems in the book as starting points. Look at form, style, theme and subject matter. Take one or more of these elements from any poem and use it as a model for the children's own poems. Show them, by example, that a poem doesn't have to be written from the beginning to the end – if you've got a good line, then write it down and build the poem around it. Encourage them to read their poems aloud. If the poem sounds right, then it's a winner – if it has jagged edges, words that don't fit, sounds that don't gel, then it needs working on, and 'working on it' is what the craft of writing poetry is all about.

Notes on Poems

Best Friend – Judith Nicholls **page 22**

Read the poem through aloud. Find the rhymes and the rhythm. Talk about the feelings generated in the poem. Work as individuals to write two verses, using the same rhyming pattern and rhythm. Stick to the same theme for accessibility.

Poetry Jump-up – John Agard **page 23**

A brilliant poem for talking about poetry! Absolutely full of metaphors – explore them and get the children to decide what each means. Read the poem aloud with exuberance and plenty of vitality.

Voices in my Head – Judith Nicholls **page 24**

Talk about what the poem means. Practise reading it with two voices. Discuss how we are influenced by the voices in our heads. Write poems along the same lines.

Timothy – Gina Douthwaite **page 25**

Read the poem aloud. Notice the alliteration. The clever bit about this poem is the play on words at the end, making the 'upside-down' work in two ways. Find another poem with lots of alliteration; write one like it.

My Eyes Are Watering – Trevor Harvey **page 26**

Read the poem silently, then talk about what it means. Try to get a consensus of opinion – has the poet *really* got a cold or is he... perhaps, crying? What, do the children think, makes him want to cry? And why can't he admit it?

Shame – Tracey Blance **page 27**

Read the poem silently. Talk about the 'harmless fun' and the 'thoughtless grin'. Have the children ever felt like this themselves? When? Write poems about when the children themselves have been thoughtless.

No Ordinary Day – Moira Andrew **page 28**

Read the poem aloud, a different voice each verse. Look for the words that *really* tell the story. Pick out the strongest word in each verse. What does the poet mean by 'the village held its breath' and 'inched round the corner'? Can the children find any more metaphors in the poem? What does the poem *mean* to them?

Safe Crossing – Bryony Doran **page 29**

Compare this poem with the poem 'No Ordinary Day' by Moira Andrew. Apart from the obvious, what differences are there between the poems? What is each of them telling? Write a group poem about the aftermath of a sad event.

What Next? – Judith Nicholls **page 30**

Read the poem aloud, a different voice for each verse. Does it describe the children's own experiences of boredom? The poem is a syllabic cinquain. Each verse has: first line – two syllables, second line – four syllables, third line – six syllables, fourth line – eight syllables, last line – two syllables. Write individual poems, about any subject, using this form.

Days – Brian Moses **page 31**

How far does this poem let the children relive their own experience of holidays – days that race by because they're having such a good time? What do the children think of the idea of being able to save days up? Look for similes and metaphors in the poem.

Hiawatha's Childhood – Henry Wadsworth Longfellow (1807 – 1882) **page 32**

This is only a short excerpt from a classic American poem. Read it with the children so that they can 'catch' the rhythm. Dig out a copy of the whole narrative poem and share it with them over a period of time. Get them to write a small piece of poetry about their childhood, using the same form.

Holiday in Colour – Moira Andrew **page 34**

Read the poem out loud together. What do you notice? Which are the key words? It is no accident that they are alliterative, and that they change sequence. The shape of the poem also makes a pleasing pattern on the page. What kinds of feelings does the poem stir in the children? Why?

My Street Is Different at Night! – Ian Souter **page 35**

Practise reading this poem aloud, then set it so that each of four small groups or individuals has one verse each. As each verse is read aloud, the other verses could be whispered quietly 'behind' the current verse, so that the children are orchestrating it with their voices. This should give the reading a magical, mysterious quality. Set the children the task of finding another poem to read aloud and present like this.

Eldorado – Edgar Allan Poe (1809 – 1849) **page 36**

This poem is about the legendary fictitious place abounding in gold – or is it? *El Dorado* can be a metaphor for 'all that you dream of'. What do the children feel? Look for 'The Raven' and 'Annabel Lee', by the same American poet, and get the children to try and work out how to identify a poem by this poet.

Stormy Temper – Ian Souter **page 37**

Read the poem silently, then read it again, all together, aloud. This poem is full of metaphors – how many can the children find? How well do they think the poem describes a storm? Write storm poems that contain at least one metaphor.

From a Railway Carriage – Robert Louis Stevenson (1850 – 1894) **page 38**

This would be an excellent poem for performance, it has such a tight rhyming pattern and such a fast rhythm. The children need to make the pace and the rhythm follow the steam train on its journey. Set it with both solos and choruses, so that you get a good mix of sound.

Big Fears – John Rice **page 39**

Read the poem aloud to the children, and let them read it through for themselves. What is the poem trying to tell them? What *big fears* do the children have? Are they real or imagined? Does it make any difference whether they are real or imagined? Write poems entitled 'My Big Fear'.

Sun Candle – John Rice **page 40**

Appreciate the words that this poem uses. Pick out the words that the children think are most effective. Look for alliteration, look for metaphor; describe light in the form of a poem.

A Cook's Tour of Word Processing – Alan Brown **page 41**

This is a clever play on words, mixing a food processor with a word processor. Ask how the poet creates the idea of mixing the language with a food processor, rather than mixing ingredients. Working as a group, have the children make their own language poem, using the same idea, and working towards a play on words.

Alien Nightmare – Mike Hoy **page 42**

This poem is about what aliens from Mars might think of humans. Use it as a stepping-off point to talk about issues that worry the children. Create a poem along the same lines, with the aliens posing the questions about the humans.

Market Razzle-Dazzle – Irene Yates **page 43**

Have children read a line each; they must keep up the quick pace and rhythm, in true market-vendor style. Get them to look for the rhyming pattern. Talk about collective nouns – these are all made up by the poet. Encourage them to look for *real* collective nouns. Make up some of your own and write a poem with them.

Stadium Wood – Irene Rawnsley **page 44**

Every child knows that feeling of pretending to be someone you're not when you know nobody can see you. How far do they think this poem goes in describing their own feelings? What is it that makes the poem end on such an up-beat? Encourage the children to learn the poem by heart and perform it with as much gusto as they can, to feel the rise in self-esteem it gives them.

In the Swim – Trevor Harvey **page 45**

Read this poem aloud. The poem is neat and quick and makes a joke. What kind of responses can the children make to it? Why do they like it? Write a poem like it.

Left Back – Trevor Harvey **page 46**

This poem has a joke at the heart of it. Everyone identifies with the one rejected – but it's funny when they find out that it's the practice ball not a player. When you know this, you can go back to the beginning and the words have a different meaning. At first sight you think they're metaphorical, but by the end you know they're literal. Is this what makes the joke?

My Dad Is Very Keen on Sport – Trevor Harvey **page 47**

This poem can tell the children about *irony.* Look for the part where the poem rhymes – this has the effect of speeding up the words. Get the children to write a poem that begins without rhyming, then has a rhyming list, then slows down without rhyme again.

Red Card – Moira Andrew **page 48**

Notice how there are no finite verbs in this poem – only participles. Talk about this with the children; it wouldn't be acceptable as prose because there would be no 'proper sentences'. What makes it work in a poem? Look for good, strong adjectives and nouns. Have the children write a verse of a poem with no finite verbs.

Ten Things to Do with a Frisbee – Moira Andrew **page 49**

Notice the rhyming pattern: each pair of lines rhymes. Use the *ten things to do* device to write poems in rhyming couplets about a chosen subject.

Space Probe – Trevor Harvey **page 50**

Notice the device of the repeat of the first line, and the fact that the end of verse one rhymes with verse two. It isn't always necessary to make verses rhyme *inside* themselves. Work as a group to write a poem that does the same. Make sure that the rhythm is the same for each verse.

Blast-off! – Moira Andrew **page 51**

Compare this poem with the poem 'Red Card' by the same poet. How many devices can the children find that she has used which are the same? Get them to look for the rhyming pattern. Write a *ten, nine, eight,* etc. poem.

Seeing St*rs – Gina Douthwaite **page 52**

Notice how the poet has used asterisks to form stars where there are *a*'s in the words. How effective do the children find this? What kind of 'feel' does the poem have – how does it appeal to their senses?

Our Holiday on the Moon – Irene Yates **page 53**

How far does the poet produce visual pictures in the children's minds? Which pictures appeal to them most? Get the children to look, and listen, for the rhyming pattern. Write poetry or prose explaining the rules of the games 'Jump the crater' and 'Float past a star'.

Escape at Bedtime – Robert Louis Stevenson (1850 – 1894) **page 54**

Think in terms of 'space'. Read this poem with the more contemporary ones in the book about space and compare them. Robert Louis Stevenson died in 1894, so his concept of space would have been very different from ours. Get the children to discuss this and how the times have made a difference to poetry.

Maybe There's a New World ... – Irene Yates **page 55**

Look for the various devices in this poem. The first is the repetition of the words 'In space maybe there's a new world ...' Look for instances of alliteration. Look for instances of what's normal for earth being turned upside down for space. Write poems with a repeating line – create one, or use the one from this poem.

In Our Family – Ian Souter page 56

Wonderful metaphors in this poem! What does it mean *Dad is hree Shredded Wheat* ? What does it mean *Mum is ... the warmth inside my duvet*? Write poems using metaphors like this, about colleagues, friends or family.

My Little Sister – Moira Andrew page 57

What feelings does this poem promote in the children? Does it make them remember being small, and not quite in control? This is a good example of a poem creating a mood – can the children explain and describe that mood?

My Gran – Moira Andrew page 58

Read aloud, with individuals reading each separate line and one voice reading the 'My Gran was' and 'She was' and the last two lines. Talk about the poem after reading it aloud two or three times; each line has a kind of experience written into it. Describe, in the children's own words, what the Gran was really like.

Oh Gran! – Irene Yates page 59

This is a gran who gives her grandchildren a hard time. But, when they try to take her advice, everything goes wrong. Why do the children think this is? What does the 'Yeah, yeah' mean at the end? Write poems about how the world has changed in the last twenty or thirty years.

Granny Is a Sprinter – Trevor Harvey page 60

Compare this poem with the poem 'My Gran' by Moira Andrew. How do the grandmothers themselves compare? How do the words of the poems compare? Write poems about an ideal grandmother.

Grandpa – Moira Andrew page 61

This poem has a repeating phrase – *Our Grandpa used to ...* From the poem, can the children identify the kind of 'time' and culture the poet is talking about? How does the poet feel about the grandfather? What feelings does the poem arouse in the children?

Mum's Infallible Method ... – Judith Nicholls page 62

This poem is different in that its title is somewhat longer than the poem itself. Which bit do the children think is really the poem? Or are they both the poem? Would the poem work without the title? The abruptness of the verse is what makes it funny. Can the children write a humorous verse of their own?

Feeling Peckish – Irene Rawnsley page 63

This poem rhymes but not quite where you expect it to. But it still scans. Talk to the children about scansion – a poem can be a poem without any rhyme, but it *has* to scan, the words *have* to *fit* together to sound right. What do the children think of the *idea* of this poem? Write poems like it, about someone who turned into something else.

True Confession – Irene Rawnsley page 64

Definitely a confession – feel the ring of guilt even though the poet says she doesn't care. The poem is written as though the poet is just telling the reader or listener something, it's very conversational. Write a conversational poem in the same way. Set it into four stanzas.

Children Menu – Gina Douthwaite page 65

Notice not *'children's menu'*. Each item on the menu is a play on words, and there's a nice little rider at the bottom. Can the children add to the menu?

A–Z of People and Party Food – Moira Andrew page 66

Notice the a, b, c – all the way through the alphabet and no words repeated. Set the children to write an A–Z poem of their own.

Ice Cream – Irene Yates page 67

Read this poem aloud. The poem has an interesting pattern. The second and fifth lines rhyme, the third and fourth lines rhyme. Notice the rhythm also. Look for alliteration. The words the poet uses are all words that 'tempt' the listener. Notice that the description isn't just about taste. Write a poem using the same pattern.

Did You See? – Jean Kenward page 68

Have the children read this poem, silently, to themselves. What picture does it bring into their minds? It talks about Winter as if it were a man – which metaphors give the reader this idea? Can the children see the contrast between the first verse and the second?

Windy Nights – Robert Louis Stevenson (1850 – 1894) page 69

This is a very famous ghost poem. Ask the children to read it aloud, as a group, then break it down into solo parts and choruses. You could make a good presentation of it by emphasising the ghost and the haunting, and getting some of the children to make a background of their voices, whispering as the wind. Can the children *hear* how the rhyme and the rhythm fit the theme of the poem?

A Rhyme – Anonymous **page 70**

This old traditional rhyme is a play on words and a good introduction to a discussion of homophones. Make sure the children understand the two words that sound the same – whether and weather – and then get them to learn the poem and recite it by heart. It needs lots of 'attack' to make it work well.

Five Answers to the Question... – Judith Nicholls **page 71**

Many, many similes and metaphors in this set of answers. Ask the children to read each part carefully and pick out the phrases they like best. Can they explain what those phrases mean? Why do they like them? What pictures do they conjure up? Write poems answering the question 'Where did Winter go?'

Winter – William Shakespeare (1564 - 1616) **page 72**

Look for the rhyme, rhythm and alliteration. The children may struggle to understand some of the lines but could probably have a good 'stab' at them. Read the poem aloud, together, several times. What do they like about it? Why? What kind of mood does the poem create? Apart from the poet's name, how would the children recognise this as an 'old' poem?

Christmas Shopping in our High Street – Judith Nicholls **page 73**

The poet has chosen her words very carefully to reveal moods and atmospheres. Notice how both change between day and night. The contrast between the two stanzas makes the poem work. Write a group poem that has the same kind of contrast.

Rubric for Enjoying a Firework Display – Irene Yates **page 74**

Each stanza of this poem follows the pattern of a Haiku – three lines of five syllables, seven syllables and then five syllables. The fact that there are five stanzas makes it balance. Write a poem using the same form.

Shopping List for a Firework Display – Irene Yates **page 75**

Read this poem alongside the poem 'Market Razzle-Dazzle' by the same poet(see page 43). She has used the same idea of collective nouns to describe the items for the firework display. How well do the children think the collective nouns fit the fireworks? Write your own collective noun firework poem.

Bonfire Party – Irene Yates **page 76**

Get the feel of the rhythm and the rhyming pattern. The poem needs lots of pace to be presented orally. Because of the vocabulary and the rhythm, it would be a good poem for a group of children to record on to a cassette, reciting one verse.

Low Owl – John Rice **page 77**

This poem is called a *univolic.* A univolic uses only one of the five vowels; in this case the vowel is 'o'. Notice how the poet has managed to create a strong atmosphere, despite the constraints of the form. Give the children the opportunity to write a univolic of their own. Give them plenty of time: it's *very* hard work! Start by just trying a single sentence.

Polar Bear – John Rice **page 78**

A kind of melancholy song. What is it that gives it this mood? What does the poet mean when he describes the polar bears as 'pillows on a white sheet'? What is the 'ancient song'? Why do the polar bears have 'great, timeless eyes'? Encourage the children to give their own interpretations of these phrases. Allow them to feel comfortable in their own personal responses.

The Eagle – Alfred, Lord Tennyson (1809 – 1892) **page 79**

The children might look at this poem and shout 'haiku'. But they would be wrong. Each line of the poem has eight syllables, each stanza has three lines which rhyme and the poem has a fair amount of alliteration. Can they write a poem themselves using this form?

The Aquarium – Brian Moses **page 80**

Read the poem aloud. Ask the children to give their immediate response to it. Then ask them to read it to themselves, and see if they notice more play on words that they didn't notice the first time. Write a word play animal poem.

Skunks – Brian Moses **page 81**

This is the poet making a case for the poor old skunk. How good a job does he do? Do the children feel sorry for the skunk? Do they understand him? What words does the poet use to convey the feelings of the skunk?

Dragons' Wood – Brian Moses **page 82**

Lots of ideas in this poem – of course, dragons don't exist – or do they? Given the evidence of the poem, perhaps they do. What do the children think? Read the poem aloud, read it silently, then aloud again. The children can play with the words on their tongues. What response does the poem arouse in them?

Midnight Badgers – Alan Brown **page 83**

What a wonderful picture the poet conjures up of the badgers, from the clatter of the claws, to their 'over-stuffed legs' and 'black barred heads'. Ask the children to pick out all the strong descriptive phrases, and to interpret them. Practise reading the poem aloud.

Akol and the Giraffe – Adapted from legend by Irene Yates **page 84**

Read the narrative poem aloud to the children before helping them to read it for themselves. Talk about what happens in the poem and which bits give the narrative its poetic feel. Get the chldren to write their own narrative poems, from the point of view of Akol. If you or your pupils would like to know more about Schools under the Trees in the Sudan, please contact the publisher. Irene Yates thanks The Revd. Joseph Ayok-Loewenberg for giving his permission for her to adapt his narrative.

How the Tortoise Got its Shell – Judith Nicholls **page 86**

A story poem that's full of information. Ask the children to look for the rhyming pattern and also to notice the vocabulary and to ask themselves what it means, eg 'the feathered', 'hooters', 'squawkers', etc. Work out what makes the form 'story poem' different from simply 'story'. Rewrite the information in the poem in narrative form.

Hurt No Living Thing – Christina Rossetti (1830 – 1894) **page 88**

Read this poem alongside some of the poems on the topic of animals in this section and compare their themes. Do the children recognise this as an 'older' poem? What makes it different from the contemporary ones, in terms of language?

Insect – Judith Nicholls **page 89**

This is an acrostic poem, where the initial letter of each line spells, downwards, the title of the poem. Write an acrostic poem about other animals. Beware of using the same word twice – and try not to include the title word in the body of the poem.

Advice about Dogs – Irene Rawnsley page 90

Get the children to work out which proverbs the poet has actually made use of. Look up some further proverbs and get the children to make up their own new 'dog' proverbs from them.

Jabberwocky – Lewis Carroll (1832 – 1898) page 91

Read the poem through with the children several times and then spend time interpreting it. Get the children to write their own versions, choosing their own vocabulary – either 'real' words or their own 'made up' words. They should be able to decide which words are nouns, which adjectives, which verbs, etc.

Death – Gina Douthwaite page 92

A shape poem. Why do the children think the poet has chosen this shape? It is *symbolic* of the theme of the poem. Get the children to look for internal rhyme and alliteration. Have them read the poem aloud and play with the phrases on their tongues. Read the poem in small groups, each child taking a sentence at a time.

Births/Marriages/Deaths – Gina Douthwaite page 93

You may need to acquaint the children with the Births/Marriages/Deaths columns from the newspapers to show them how this form has been taken over by the poet to humorous effect. Choose another type of animal and write new poems using the same form.

Lambs – Gina Douthwaite page 94

Do the children know how lambs skip and bounce and jump? Can they describe the way the lambs move, in their own words? Get them to compare their own words with the poem. How has the poet captured the *exact* movements of the spring lambs? What do the children think of the imagery such as 'newly knit lambs' and 'milky mum'?

Nick's Cat – Gina Douthwaite page 95

This poem cries out to be read aloud, fast. Read it all together first, then let the children read it in groups of three, taking a line at a time, in order, and using the alliteration to its very best effect. What do the children particularly like about the poem?

Seagulls in the City – Irene Yates **page 96**

Look for alliteration, metaphor, simile and notice how the poem begins and ends at exactly the same place so that it keeps going round and round. The poem changes pace at 'Where is the sea in all this?' Why do the children think this is? What feelings do they get from the first part of the poem and then from the second?

Up in the Air – Moira Andrew **page 98**

This is an acrostic poem where the initial letters spell the word: butterfly. Each phrase describes the butterfly and captures the lightness of its movement. Have the children choose their own creatures and write acrostic poems.

One Wicked Weasel – Moira Andrew **page 99**

There is lots of alliteration in this poem. Look at the form of the poem. It is written in rhyming couplets. Arm the children with dictionaries and thesauruses and write a class poem using this form, following this pattern.

How Doth the Little Crocodile – Lewis Carroll (1832 – 1898) **page 100**

This poem sets out to show the crocodile in a good light but ends with a kind of 'nature red in tooth and claw' twist. What do the children like about it? Can they write their own poems, using this form, about an animal – showing it in its glory and then giving it a predatory twist at the end?

The Silent Snake – Anonymous **page 101**

This old, traditional poem has an unusual rhyming scheme that the children should notice. Ask them also to look for instances of alliteration. Write a group poem, using exactly the same rhyming scheme and the same rhythm. You could write a poem about modern transport that might fit these patterns well.

Best Friend

When there's just one square
of chocolate left ...
she shares,
she gives me half.

When thunder growls like an angry bear
and I shiver and shake
beneath my chair...
she won't laugh.

When I'm grumpy or cross
or spotty or sad,
when I whine or boss ...
she stays.

When things aren't fair
and I hurt inside,
when I just want to hide ...
she's there,
always.

Judith Nicholls

Poetry Jump-up

Tell me if Ah seeing right
Took a look down de street

Words dancin
words dancin
till dey sweat
words like fishes
jumpin out a net
words wild and free
joinin de poetry revelry
words back to back
words belly to belly

'Come on everybody
come and join de poetry band
dis is poetry carnival
dis is poetry bacchanal
when inspiration call
take yu pen in yu hand
if yu don't have a pen
take yu pencil in yu hand
if yu don't have a pencil
what the hell
so long as de feeling start to swell
just shout de poem out

Words jumpin off de page
tell me if Ah seein right
words like birds
jumpin out a cage
take a look down de street

Words shakin dey waist
words shakin dey bum
words wit black skin
words wit white skin
words wit brown skin
words wit no skin at all
words huggin up words
an sayin I want to be a poem today
rhyme or no rhyme
I is a poem today
I mean to have a good time

Words feeling hot hot hot
big words feelin hot hot hot
lil words feelin hot hot hot
even sad words can't help
tappin dey toe
to de riddum of de poetry band

Dis is poetry carnival
dis is poetry bacchanal
so come on everybody
join de celebration
all yu need is plenty perspiration
an a little inspiration
plenty perspiration
an a little inspiration

John Agard

Voices in my Head

I daren't!

You can do it.

I can't!

You can do it.

What if ... ?

You can do it.

Perhaps ...

You can do it.

DARE I do it?

You can do it.

Well, MAYBE I should ...

You can do it.

I DID IT!

I said you could do it.

I knew I would!

Judith Nicholls

Timothy

Tipple, topple Timothy
took a train to town,
travelled to the terminus
upside-down.

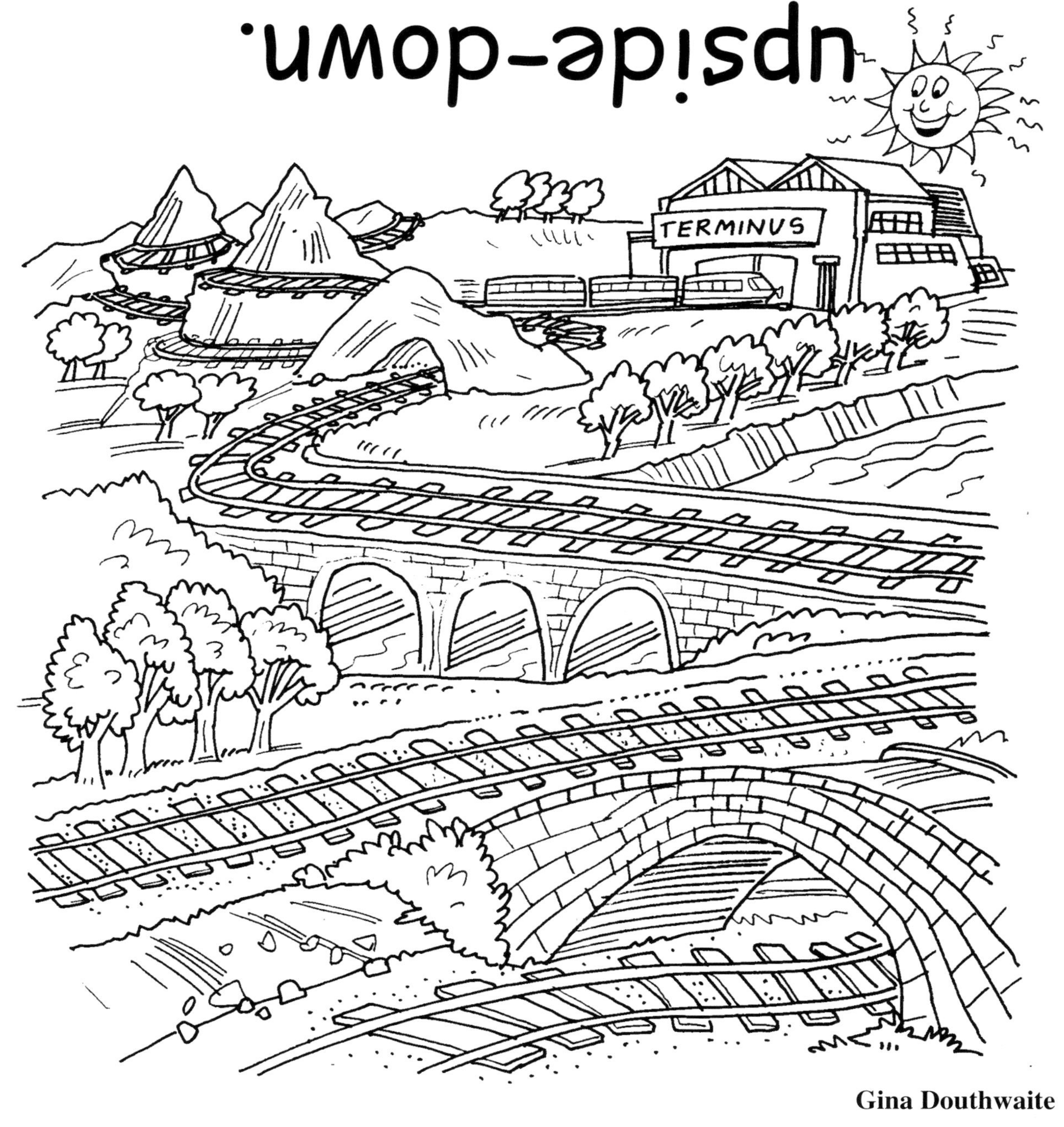

Gina Douthwaite

My Eyes Are Watering

I've got a cold
And that is why
My eyes are watering.

It's nothing to do
With getting caught
When I had planned
To SMASH
The rounders ball
SO FAR
That it would go
Into PERMANENT ORBIT
Round the school.
It would've done, too –
If Lucy Smith
Hadn't RUSHED
To catch it.

'Look at Trevor –
He's having a cry!'
Not true.
I've got a cold
And THAT is why
My eyes are watering.

OK?

Trevor Harvey

Shame

There's a girl at school
we teased today;
made jokes, called her names.
My friends all laughed,
called it harmless fun,
said it was just a game.

Now I'm at home
feeling horrid inside,
long gone that thoughtless grin.
How will I face her
tomorrow at school?
I wish I hadn't joined in.

Tracey Blance

No Ordinary Day

It was the saddest day
we had ever known.
No pushing or shoving,
everyone unusually
well-behaved.

Assembly, no teachers,
just us listening, the head
holding back tears, trying
to tell us how she felt about
the accident.

Playtime, but nobody
played. We whispered,
watching the empty road,
where no-one walked this
summer morning.

The village held its breath.
We stood by the gate, cooks,
cleaners, caretaker, teachers,
children. We waited together
in silence.

Then, 'He's coming! Adrian's
coming!' one of the little ones
called. Glittering like glass,
a long black car, inched
round the corner.

In the back, a small coffin,
buried under a mound of
flowers. Then came the cars
full of familiar people in
unfamiliar black.

They slid past the school.
'A five-minute run-around,
then inside!' the duty teacher
said. Released, we tumbled on
to the grass.

The day struggled back to
nearly-normal. At home-time,
parents grabbed our hands
and the ice-cream van had
few customers.

Moira Andrew

Safe Crossing

My friend got run over
He broke both arms
And a leg
So he can't use crutches
He has a wheel chair
And his mum has to push him
Home from school

He used to laugh at us
For crossing at the school patrol
'My mum never picks me up'
He used to boast
But now she does
And he goes straight home
While we play footie in the park
Until it's time for tea
I like it being alive

Bryony Doran

What Next?

Boredom
hangs around us
like a grey net curtain,
fogging our view, shutting out all
sunlight.

Boredom
is a blank sheet
waiting to be printed ...
but we have no pen, no pencil,
no ink.

Boredom
closes in; slick,
surreptitious burglar,
grasping with both hands. A dull thief
of time.

Judith Nicholls

Days

Days fly by on holidays,
they escape like birds
released from cages.
What a shame you can't buy
tokens of time, save them up
and lengthen the good days,
or maybe you could tear out time
from days that drag, then pay it back
on holidays, wild days,
days you wish would last forever.
You could wear these days with pride,
fasten them like poppies to your coat,
or keep them in a tin, like sweets,
a confection of days
to be held on the tongue
and tasted, now and then.

Brian Moses

Hiawatha's Childhood

(extract from The Story of Hiawatha)

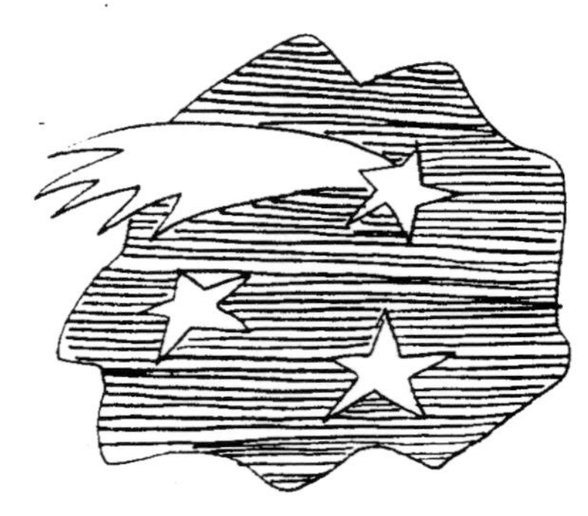

By the shores of Gitche Gumee,
By the shining Big-Sea-Water,
Stood the wigwam of Nokomis,
Daughter of the Moon, Nokomis.
Dark behind it rose the forest,
Rose the black and gloomy pine-trees,
Rose the firs with cones upon them;
Bright before it beat the water,
Beat the clear and sunny water,
Beat the shining Big-Sea-Water.

There the wrinkled, old Nokomis
Nursed the little Hiawatha,
Rocked him in his linden cradle,
Bedded soft in moss and rushes,
Safely bound with reindeer sinews;
Stilled his fretful wail by saying,
'Hush! the Naked Bear will get thee!'
Lulled him into slumber, singing,
'Ewa-yea! my little owlet!
Who is this, that lights the wigwam?
With his great eyes lights the wigwam?
Ewa-yea! my little owlet!'

Many things Nokomis taught him
Of the stars that shine in heaven;
Showed him Ishkoodah, the comet,
Ishkoodah, with fiery tresses;
Showed the Death-Dance of the spirits.
Warriors with their plumes and war-clubs,
Flaring far away to northward
In the frosty nights of Winter;
Showed the broad, white road in heaven,
Pathway of the ghosts, the shadows,
Running straight across the heavens,
Crowded with the ghosts, the shadows.

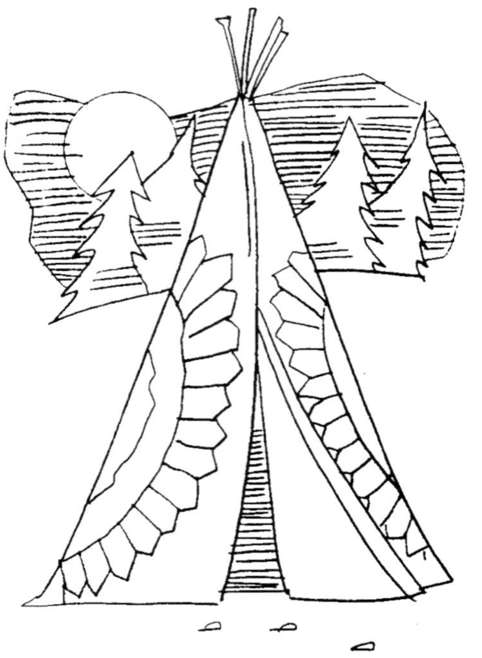

At the door on Summer evenings
Sat the little Hiawatha;
Heard the whispering of the pine-trees,
Heard the lapping of the water,
Sounds of music, words of wonder;
'Minne-wawa!' said the pine-trees,
'Mudway-aushka!' said the water.

Saw the fire-fly, Wah-wah-taysee,
Flitting through the dusk of evening,
With the twinkle of its candle
Lighting up the brakes and bushes,
And he sang the song of children,
Sang the song Nokomis taught him:

'Wah-wah-taysee, little fire-fly,
Little, flitting, white-fire insect,
Little, dancing, white-fire creature,
Light me with your little candle,
Ere upon my bed I lay me,
Ere in sleep I close my eyelids!'
Saw the moon rise from the water,
Rippling, rounding from the water,
Saw the flecks and shadows on it
Whispered, 'What is that, Nokomis?'
And the good Nokomis answered:
'Once a warrior, very angry,
Seized his grandmother, and threw her
Up into the sky at midnight;
Right against the moon he threw her;
Tis her body that you see there.'
Saw the rainbow in the heaven,
In the eastern sky the rainbow,
Whispered, 'What is that, Nokomis?'
And the good Nokomis answered:
Tis the heaven of flowers you see there;
All the wild-fowers of the forest,
All the lilies of the prairie,
When on earth they fade and perish,
Blossom in that heaven above us.'
When he heard the owls at midnight,
Hooting, laughing in the forest,
'What is that?' he cried in terror;
'What is that,' he said, 'Nokomis?'
And the good Nokomis answered:
'That is but the owl and owlet,
Talking in their native language,
Talking, scolding at each other.'

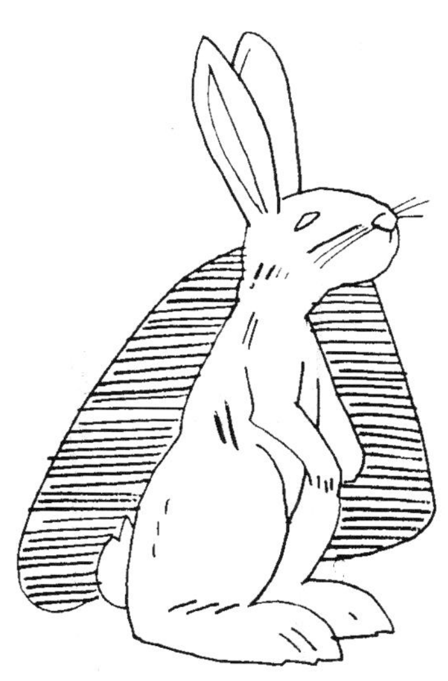

Then the little Hiawatha
Learned of every bird its language,
Learned their names and all their secrets,
How they built their nests in Summer,
Where they hid themselves in Winter,
Talked with them whene'er he met them,
Called them 'Hiawatha's Chickens.'
Of all beasts he learned the language,
Learned their names and all their secrets,
How the beavers built their lodges,
Where the squirrels hid their acorns,
How the reindeer ran so swiftly,
Why the rabbit was so timid,
Talked with them whene'er he met them,
Called them 'Hiawatha's Brothers.'

Henry Wadsworth Longfellow

Holiday in Colour

sky
sun
sea
sand
Listen to that scarlet band!

sand
sky
sun
sea
Feel blue breezes wild and free!

sea
sand
sky
sun
Taste pink-striped ices on your tongue!

sun
sea
sand
sky
Watch white-winged seagulls dip and fly!

Smell salt-rimmed waves at every turn
where golden sand makes bare feet burn.

Swim and splash and race and run
under sapphire sky and yellow sun!

Moira Andrew

My Street Is Different at Night!

My street is different at night
when darkness and silence arrive
to smother and cover
everything in sight.

Then:
trees become long, sweeping hands
searching for something dropped
and cars sit like watchdogs
huddling together for warmth.

And:
houses change into frightening witches
with their great, black pointed hats
and ghostly white breath
drifting slowly up into the sky.

While:
the road is a thick snake of dark tarmac
slithering off to lose itself in the night
and only in the early morning
will it find its way back again.

Ian Souter

Eldorado

Gaily bedight,
A gallant knight,
In sunshine and in shadow,
Had journeyed long,
Singing a song,
In search of Eldorado.

But he grew old –
This knight so bold –
And o'er his heart a shadow
Fell, as he found
No spot of ground
That looked like Eldorado.

And, as his strength
Failed him at length,
He met a pilgrim shadow –
'Shadow,' said he,
'Where can it be –
This land of Eldorado?'

'Over the Mountains
Of the Moon,
Down the Valley of the Shadow,
Ride, boldly ride,'
The shade replied,
'If you seek for Eldorado!'

Edgar Allan Poe

Stormy Temper

Yesterday I woke
to find my bedroom window
shivering on the wall
while outside,
as the rain clapped loudly,
cars sprayed their way along my street.

Yesterday I walked outside
and immediately the cold licked my face
with its frozen tongue,
while the wind pushed past
to chase litter down the street.
Behind me the garden fence
began breaking dancing over the grass
and the washing line skipped across a bruised sky.

Yesterday I watched,
as the weather got really angry
and ripped the roof off a nearby house
as if it were made of wrapping paper.
Then so easily, as if it were a toy,
it toppled a lorry on to its side,
leaving only the wipers
waving frantically for help.

But today the weather
sent fingers of light
to creep into my bedroom
and offer a warming hand.
It seemed to be an apology
for yesterday's stormy temper.

Ian Souter

From a Railway Carriage

Faster than fairies, faster than witches,
Bridges and houses, hedges and ditches;
And charging along like troops in a battle,
All through the meadows the horses and cattle:
All of the sights of the hill and the plain
Fly as thick as driving rain;
And ever again, in the wink of an eye,
Painted stations whistle by.

Here is a child who clambers and scrambles,
All by himself and gathering brambles;
Here is a tramp who stands and gazes;
And there is the green for stringing the daisies!
Here is a cart run away in the road
Lumping along with man and load;
And here is a mill, and there is a river:
Each a glimpse and gone for ever!

Robert Louis Stevenson

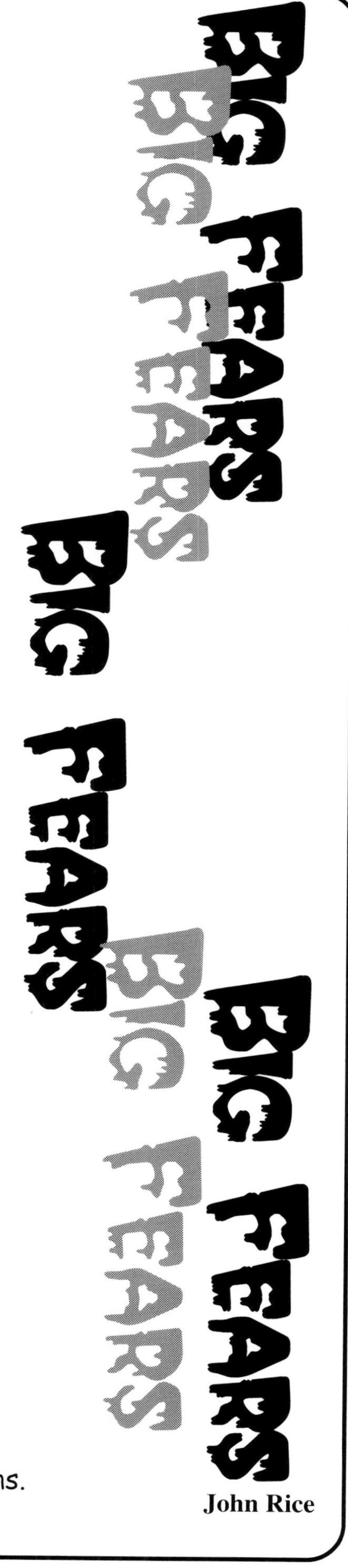

Twenty-five feet above Sian's house
hangs a thick wire cable
that droops and sags between
two electricity pylons.
A notice says it carries 320,000 volts
from one metallic scarecrow to the next,
then on to the next and the next
right across the countryside to the city.
The cable sways above Sian's council house
making her radio crackle and sometimes
making her telly go on the blink.

If it's a very windy night
Sian gets frightened because
she thinks the cable might snap,
fall onto the roof and electrocute
everyone as they sleep.
This is Sian's big fear.

Outside Matthew's bedroom there is
a tall tree – taller than the house.
In summer it is heavy with huge leaves.
In winter it stands lonely as a morning moon.

On a windy night Matthew worries
that the tree might be blown down
and crash through his bedroom window.
It would certainly kill him ... and his cat
if it was sleeping under the bed
where it usually goes.
This is Matthew's big fear.

Outside Sam's bedroom there's nothing
but a pleasant view; meadows, hedges, sheep
and some distant gentle hills.
There's nothing sinister, nothing frightening,
nothing to worry about.

But at night, in the dark, Sam thinks
the darting shapes on the ceiling
are really the shadows
of a ghost's great cold hands and
that the night noises made by the water pipes
are the screeches and groans of attic skeletons.

John Rice

Sun Candle

The sun is like a searchlight;
  it scorns, it scalds, it scorches.
The light of stars is dimmer,
  a swarm of distant torches.

The planets shed their lamplight,
  ashen grey or pepper red:
the moonglow, pale as snowdrops,
  scatters petals on my bed.

John Rice

A Cook's Tour of Word Processing

When Mum goes out I play in the kitchen
With her word processor.

I slice words into pie - ces
With her word processor.

I up my mix words
With her word processor.

I
shred
my
sensible
sentences
With her word processor.

I liquidise the luscious language
With her word processor.

I make messy metaphors all over the kitchen
With her word processor.

And when Mum comes back I say,
'It was nothing to do with me.'

Alan Brown

Alien Nightmare

Do you believe in aliens?
And can you tell me why
they poison all the air
and cause the land to die?
The little Martian Spoglets
lying in their beds
bite their thirty fingers
with mouths in both their heads

Do they really cut down forests
to build the noisy motorway?
Do they really eat dead animals
and keep kids in class all day?
They've heard a horror story
and the shadows as they creep
make them think the monsters
will grab them as they sleep.

Do they really let their people starve
and hunt rabbit, deer and gnus?
Do they slaughter all the animals
or lock them up in zoos?
They've been watching sci-fi films
shown on M T V
about some scarey aliens
that look like you and me.

Mike Hoy

Market Razzle-Dazzle

Roll up! Roll up!
Come here and buy!

A chuckle of laughter –
A tearful of cry!
An armful of sorrow –
A goodness of blest –
A comfort of caring –
A joggin' of zest!
A smile for a sweetheart –
A kiss for a fall –
A ha-porth of blushing –
A teasing of tall!
A green-eye of jealous –
A pinching of spite –
A glowing of humour –
A powerful of might!
A flutter of kindness –
A smidgin of cope –
A warming of friendship –
A heartful of hope!
A fluster of anxious –
A thumping of fear –
A ferment of eager –
A softness of dear!
A loyal of loving –
A quiver of sigh –
A lively of learn –
An excitement of try!
The Market of Life's full of
  Where? What? And Why?

Roll up! Roll up!
Come here and buy!

RAZZLE-
DAZZLE
RAZZLE-
DAZZLE
RAZZLE-
DAZZLE

Irene Yates

Stadium Wood

Out in the woods today
the trees are roaring like a crowd
watching me play football,
waving their leaves to cheer me on
as I score goal after goal.

I slip past the opposition, dribbling, dodging;
nobody has a hope of stopping me.
Another goal!
The trees punch the air with their branches;
this boy must be picked for England soon;
he's SENSATIONAL!

Irene Rawnsley

In the Swim

Can anybody tell me why
They call this stroke
The Butterfly?

Is it that, to be effectual,
My arms and legs must look
Symmetrical?

Trevor Harvey

Left Back

Why is it
Always ME
That gets belted and booted
And treated like dirt?

I'm fed up
With everyone
Just kicking me around.
It's so deflating!

I've been with them for WEEKS,
Seen their ups and downs,
Prepared with them for Wembley.

But when it comes to the Big Occasion,
What happens? What do they think of me now?

Do they remember the battering I've had
And let me share their moment of glory?

No way!

They just say
I'm a scruffed practice ball –
And I'm not 'Match Fit'.

Trevor Harvey

My Dad Is Very Keen on Sport

My Dad may be OLD
But he's still keen on sport –
WATCHING IT is *bliss!*
So he's had installed Cable TV
To make sure he does not miss
A single
football match goal
cricketer's bowl
downhill ski
golf match tee
runner's sprint
ice-skate glint
judo throw
rower's row
rider's jump
stockcar's bump
swimmer's stroke
engine's choke
basketball score
or rugby crowd's roar!

BUT after five minutes
He falls asleep
In his armchair.

My Dad is living proof that
Although Sport may be INSPIRING
It is also VERY tiring... !

Trevor Harvey

Red Card

Twenty two lads
sprinting
for the ball,
one unbiased referee
watching
gimlet-eyed,
two unfit linesmen
puffing
on the touchline.
twenty two dads
shouting
brash encouragement,
assorted bored teachers
freezing
in the wind.

Two keen players
passing
from the wing,
one super striker
flicking
into the net,
one unlucky goalie
diving
to no avail,
one confident referee
whistling
for a GOAL!
a few away parents
thundering
their approval.

Eleven home fathers
erupting
from the touchline,
a dozen partisan parents
fighting
behind the goal,
one unruffled referee
stopping
the game abruptly,
one red card
blazing
in his hand,
two schoolboy teams
following
officials from the pitch.

Twenty two players
returning
to the showers,
one stern referee
making
an example
of twenty-odd parents
misbehaving
on the touchline,
one red card
freezing out
the 'hooligans',
a few chastened fathers
apologising
to their sons.

Moira Andrew

Ten Things to Do with a Frisbee

You can spin it in the air.
You can whizz it across a chair.

You can send it into space.
You can enter it in a race.

You can fly it above the trees.
You can float it on the breeze.

You can zip it across the sky.
You can make it soar up very high.

You can fling it over the river –
Help! You've lost track of it forever!

Moira Andrew

Space Probe

I am a Space Probe –
Sending back signals
To turn into pictures
At Mission Control;
Cameras active,
Instruments working –
A man-made machine
That is speeding to Mars.

I am a Space Probe –
Journeying onwards,
Searching for water –
That is my goal;
Seeking out planets,
Sending back details –
A machine to help Man
Find his way to the Stars.

Trevor Harvey

Blast-off!

Ten astronauts waving,
    Nine doors shutting tight.
Eight scientists counting down,
    Seven screens blinking bright.
Six boosters revving up,
    Five controls in a row.
Four rockets shuddering,
    Three head-sets saying 'Go!'
Two fuel tanks in place,
    One shuttle off to space!

BLAST-OFF!

Moira Andrew

Seeing St*rs

A pl*ce
c*lled sp*ce
*bove the sky
c*nnot be seen,
it's f*r too high,
until
*t night
it switches on
its *stro-lights
– a million

or more
like eyes
that sleep by d*y
then st*y aw*ke
to bl*ze aw*y
from dusk till d*wn
then dis*ppear
just *s the
ch*sing sun
dr*ws ne*r.

Gina Douthwaite

Our Holiday on the Moon

We went to the moon
For our holiday week,
It's cheap in the summer
That's when it's off-peak.
We stayed in a moonship,
Caravan-style.
Well, Mum said 'It's easy,
We'll give it a trial.'
It didn't have beds.
There weren't any stairs,
You just kind of floated
And didn't need chairs.
You could hang from the ceiling
By head or by heels,
Drink back-to-front,
And have upside-down meals.
The people are friendly.
Their heads are in threes.
They have hugging pads
On their elbows and knees.
Moon men and moon women
Are short, fat and round.
They laugh all the time,
Without making a sound –
But moon babies are squashy
Because of the hugs –
With sets of antennae,
A little like bugs.
They play JUMP THE CRATER
And FLOAT PAST A STAR
And they're free to fly off
But they never go far.

It's great on the moon
And we're going again –
You can come if you like –
Next year? See you then!

Irene Yates

Escape at Bedtime

The lights from the parlour and kitchen shone out
    Through the blinds and the windows and bars;
And high overhead and all moving about,
    There were thousands of millions of stars.
There ne'er were such thousands of leaves on a tree,
    Nor of people in church or the Park,
As the crowds of the stars looked down upon me,
    And that glittered and winked in the dark.

The Dog, and the Plough, and the Hunter, and all,
    And the star of the sailor, and Mars,
These shone in the sky, and the pail by the wall
    Would be half full of water and stars.
They saw me at last, and they chased me with cries,
    And they soon had me packed into bed;
But the glory kept shining and bright in my eyes,
    And the stars going round in my head.

Robert Louis Stevenson

Maybe There's a New World ...

In space
maybe there's a
new world
and the people
are green
with three heads
four eyes and
a bucket
on the end
of their nose. In
space
maybe there's a
new world
and the land is
sticky like
marmalade
and the sea is
red like
stop on the traffic
lights and
the sun beats up
instead of
down and the
wind chuckles instead
of
sighs and the
rain's made of
tears. In space
maybe there's a
new world
and the daisies
smell of new shoes
and
cornflakes taste like
a day at the seaside
and the fish fly and
the birds swim and the
elephants sing and
the zebras dance and
the monkeys go to
school and
the children have
nothing to do but play
in the trees
all day.

Irene Yates

In Our Family

In our family:

Dad is three Shredded Wheat,
he's a faded pair of jeans,
he's a winning goal at football
and he's the thunder and lightning in a storm.

In our family:

Mum is a tumbling washing machine,
she's the crunch in autumn leaves,
she's the warmth inside my duvet
and she's the 'no' you wish was a 'yes'!

In our family:

My brother Sam's a muddy wellington boot,
he's a lumpy plate of mashed potato,
he's porridge flying across the table
and he's the laughter in a game of hide and seek.

In our family:

that leaves me!
And I'm ....
not telling!!

Ian Souter

My Little Sister

They said they'd let me
hold her in the garden
for a photograph.

'Be careful,' they said.
'She's new and tiny
and very very precious.'

They sat me on a chair,
my legs dangling.
'Ready now?' they asked.

And they placed her
on my lap, wriggling and wet.
'Smile,' they said.

I tried, but it wasn't easy
to hold the baby and smile,
both at the same time.

Moira Andrew

My Gran

My Gran was
  a giggle-in-the-corner-like-a-child
          kind of Gran

She was
  a put-your-cold-hand-in-my-pocket
  a keep-your-baby-curls-in-my-locket
          kind of Gran

She was
  a make-it-better-with-a-treacle-toffee
  a what-you-need's-a-cup-of-milky-coffee
  a hurry-home-I-love-you-awfully
          kind of Gran

She was
  a butter-ball-for-your-bad-throat
  a stitch-your-doll-a-new-green-coat
  a let's-make-soapy-bubbles-float
  a hold-my-hand-I'm-seasick-in-a-boat
          kind of Gran

She was
  a toast-your-tootsies-by-the-fire
  a crack-the-wishbone-for-your-heart's-desire
  a ladies-don't-sweat-they-perspire
  a funny-old-fashioned-higgeldy-piggeldy-lady-to-admire
          kind of Gran

And this lovely grandmother
was mine, all mine!

Moira Andrew

Oh Gran!

My gran says
'When I was your age
We played outside
All day long.
Hopscotch on the pavement.
Tig off ground across the kerb.
Knock the door and run.
You kids today –
You just don't know how to enjoy
    yourselves!'

We tried playing in the street
Once.
'What are you doing!
Under our feet on the pavement!'
    people yelled.
Cars and lorries tigged off ground
Across the kerb
And a stranger knocked a door and
stood and watched us.

My gran says
'When I was your age ...'
Yeah, yeah.

Irene Yates

Granny Is a Sprinter

My granny is a sprinter –
She races for the bus
And always gets to climb on board
Before the rest of us.

'You ought to run a marathon,'
A cheeky driver told her.
Gran smiled and said, 'I think I may –
When I'm a little older!'

Trevor Harvey

Grandpa

Our Grandpa
used to take us
up to the top of the house
to inspect the weather.

Our Grandpa
used to buy us
fish and chips in vinegar
for a Saturday treat.

Our Grandpa
used to give us
shiny half-crowns to spend
on anything we liked.

Our Grandpa
used to stand us
in a line for photographs
and try to make us smile.

Our Grandpa
used to tell us
the tricks he got up to
when he was a boy.

Our Grandpa
used to make us feel
the most special children
in the whole wide world.

Moira Andrew

Mum's Infallible Method for Solving Arguments about Who Gets the Biggest Slice of Cream Cake

I'll make sure
no-one loses;
you cut,
she chooses!

Judith Nicholls

Feeling Peckish

My greedy sister
turned into a hen.

She was looking in the biscuit tin
for cookies
when her fingers turned to feathers
and her arms to wings.

Now she lives in the garden
pecking cabbage stalks and things
that hens like to eat.

She claws the lawn for worms
with her scaly feet.

Irene Rawnsley

True Confession

On my birthday I wrapped
a big slice of chocolate cake
in pink paper to give
to Miss Twiglington,

but when I got to school
she was horrible to me;
'You haven't worked hard enough,
your spellings are bad,

margin crooked,
fingerprints all over'
then she ripped out the page
and made me start again. I thought

'She's not getting that cake.'
so when break time came
I ate it myself outside
and I didn't care.

Irene Rawnsley

Children Menu

BREAKFAST

Orange *Bruce*

*

Shaun Flakes

*

Meg and *Nathan* (fried)

DINNER

Helen Slice

*

Mixed *Reg*
Kate and *Sidney* pie

*

Barbara split

*

Pot of *Lee*

*

Gordonzola

TEA

Deans on toast

*

Strawberry *Sam*

*

Coca-Lola

SUPPER

Charlotte mousse
Kerry cake

*

Chilled *Liamade*

Children on this menu are all home-made

Gina Douthwaite

A–Z of People and Party Food

Alice brings Chocolate chips,
David enjoys Fish fingers,
George hogs the Ice-cream,
John knocks over the Lemonade,
Michael nibbles Oranges,
Poppy queues for Raisin'n'rum,
Stewart tastes Ugly-fruit,
Vera wants Xtra helpings,
Yasmin zips along to the party.

Moira Andrew

Ice-Cream

Ice-cream is a heavenly concoction
It's easily the most delicious fare
You can get it in all sizes
And it often has surprises
Like a strawberry you didn't know was there. (Slurp)

Ice-cream is magnificent and mellow
It has a luscious texture of its own
It's smooth and soft and silky
Also, chocolatey and milky –
And it squidges very nicely in a cone.

Ice-cream is spectacular and special
With fruit and sauce and nuts it's just sublime
(Mmmmmmm...)
It's a super-scrumptious story
And a Knickerbocker Glory
Can be polished off in record yummy time.
(Mmmmmmmm...)

Irene Yates

Did You See?

Did you hear what I heard?
A soft, soft sigh….
was it a flake of snow
fluttering by –
So light, so delicate
it could not stay
more than a moment – then
melted away?

Did you see what I saw?
Winter was there.
Cold, cold his fingertips
and crisp his hair.
Hard as a diamond
he shone, and then –
icicles in his beard –
was gone again.

Jean Kenward

Windy Nights

Whenever the moon and stars are set,
Whenever the wind is high,
All night long in the dark and wet,
A man goes riding by.
Late in the night when the fires are out,
Why does he gallop and gallop about?

Whenever the trees are crying loud,
And ships are tossed at sea,
By, on the highway, low and loud,
By at the gallop goes he.
By at the gallop he goes, and then,
By he comes back at the gallop again.

Robert Lewis Stevenson

A Rhyme

Whether the weather be fine,
    or whether the weather be not,
Whether the weather be cold,
    or whether the weather be hot,
We'll weather the weather,
    whatever the weather,
Whether we like it or not.

Anonymous

Five Answers to the Question 'Where did Winter go?'

(For the poets of Chandag Junior School, Keynsham)

**Winter slunk away
like a guilty mongrel,
brought to heel by Spring.**

**Sullen as an uninvited guest,
Winter packed his bags
and stole into the night.**

**Winter dawdled
through darkened alleyways,
past empty doorways,
over silent pavements
whitened by the moon,
then crawled,
unwillingly,
from town.**

**Winter prowled to safety,
loath to leave
as an empty-handed thief.**

**Winter fell ill,
took a chill
and did a midnight flit.
He didn't stop to pack
and no-one heard
his hoarse last word:**

I'll be back!

Judith Nicholls

Winter

When icicles hang by the wall,
And Dick the shepherd blows his nail,
And Tom bears logs into the hall,
And milk comes frozen home in pail;
When blood is nipped, and ways be foul,
Then nightly sings the staring owl.
Tu-whit, tu-who! a merry note,
While greasy Joan doth keel the pot.

When all aloud the wind doth blow,
And coughing drowns the parson's saw,
And birds sit brooding in the snow,
And Marian's nose looks red and raw,
When roasted crabs hiss in the bowl,
Then nightly sings the staring owl,
Tu-whit, tu-who! a merry note,
While greasy Joan doth keel the pot.

William Shakespeare

Christmas Shopping in our High Street

By day,
shoppers plod gloomily
from store to store.

By night,
lights shine like fallen stars
and magic's there once more.

Judith Nicholls

Rubric for Enjoying a Firework Display

Wear your wellies and
a woolly hat pulled right down
to cover your ears.

Go with your best friend
so you can have lots of fun
but don't lark about.

Make sure the fireworks
are properly organised
by someone who cares.

Look for a good spot
where you can see what's going
on. Then stand well back.

Sniff the November
frosty night, stay warm as toast
and return home safe.

Irene Yates

Shopping List for a Firework Display

One sharp, frosty night.
An inky-black midnight sky.
Several metres of safety barrier.
A circle of Catherine Wheels.
A bouquet of Crick-Crack Chrysanthemums.
A hoppit of Jumping Jacks.
A cacophony of Crackling Thunderbursts.
A zoom of Flight Rockets.
A cloudburst of Golden Showers.
A brilliance of Roman Candles.
A boom of Quadblast Bangers.
A zigzag of Singing Birds.
A torrent of Silver Fountains.
A rainbow of Bursting Violets.
One match.
15 minutes of magic.
One million Oohs and Aahs.

Irene Yates

Bonfire Party

There's a notice someone's stuck upon the lamp-post
Of a bonfire organised for our whole street.
Depending on the weather
There will be a get-together,
And they want to know what we can bring to eat.

Rashed's Mum says she will cook samosas
And make sure that he brings them piping hot.
There'll be popping corn in packets,
And potatoes in their jackets
With Caribbean drumsticks in a pot.

My Dad is making toffee covered apples
Each skewered on to little wooden sticks.
There'll be flapjacks on the menu
At the bonfire party venue
Where they've built a barbie out of some old bricks.

There are bound to be hot sausages and burgers
Sending up their scent into the night –
Sizzling and spitting
In a way that's only fitting
When a crackerjack goes off with every bite!

There'll be a huge display of whizz-bang fireworks
And rockets zooming off into the sky.
I've got a slight suspicion
That there'll be a competition
For who can make the most convincing guy.

It's going to be the greatest celebration –
All our friends and neighbours will be there!
This fifth night of November
Is the one that we'll remember –
What excitement! What a party we will share!

Irene Yates

Low Owl

– a univocalic*

Cold morn: on fork of two o'clock
owl's hoot flows from hood of wood.

Owl's song rolls from blood to brood,
owl's hoot loops onto top of town roofs,
owl's song swoops on strong doors.

Owl's slow whoop – long, forlorn –
soft flood of moon song.

**a poem which uses only one of the five vowels:
in this case the letter 'o'.*

John Rice

Polar Bear

Padding through soft snow
the polar bears are pillows on a white sheet.

They are kings of their kind,
roaming a majestic land of ice.

Who would want to destroy you
and your bright-light wasteland?
Who does not hear your ancient song?

And who cannot see the dark heat
of this past century in your great, timeless eyes?

John Rice

The Eagle

He clasps the crag with crooked hands;
Close to the sun in lonely lands,
Ring'd with the azure world, he stands.

The wrinkled sea beneath him crawls;
He watches from his mountain walls,
And like a thunderbolt he falls.

Alfred, Lord Tennyson

The Aquarium

The aquarium
was disappointing:

The dogfish
didn't bark,
the jellyfish
didn't wobble.

The sea mouse
didn't squeak,
the starfish
didn't shine.

The hermit crabs
were crabby,
the clams
clammed up,
and the plaice
stayed in one place.

But when the swordfish
attacked us,
the trigger fish
pulled out his gun,
and the piranhas invited us
to be their lunch...

we rode away fast...
on a sea horse!

Brian Moses

Skunks

You don't know what it's like
to be reviled, to be hated
or slated like we are.
You don't know what it's like
to be the subject of such bad press.
When Noah took us onto the Ark,
you should have heard the complaints.
All the other creatures moved away
to the other side of the boat
till it almost capsized,
and we were lucky to stay afloat.
Noah made us stay out on deck
after that little escapade.
But you carry on, avoid us,
shun us, run away,
steer clear, we are not
for the faint hearted or those
with sensitive noses.
We are, as you might say,
an acquired smell –
eau de skunk – you could never
bottle and sell us.
We are unique, the bad eggs,
the rotten apples,
we stink bomb your senses.
You are not impressed with us,
we will never be your dinner guests.
Somewhere out there,
in the places where bad smells linger
we wait – an explosion of unpleasantness,
no air freshener can combat.

Brian Moses

Dragons' Wood

We didn't see dragons
in Dragons' Wood
but we saw
where the dragons had been.

We saw tracks in soft mud
that could only have been scratched
by some sharp-clawed creature.

We saw scorched earth
where fiery dragon breath
had whitened everything to ash.

We saw trees burnt to charcoal.
We saw dragon dung
rolled into boulders.

And draped from a branch
we saw sloughed off skin,
scaly, still warm...

We didn't see dragons
in Dragons' Wood,
but this was the closest
we'd ever been

to believing.

Brian Moses

Midnight Badgers

In the leafy dark lane
We wait scarce breathing,
Till out of the owly night
Comes the clatter of claws
Like iron on the metal road.

Fat bear pigs,
Snorting and grunting,
Running and playing,
Boneless on over-stuffed legs,
Steel gleam of black barred heads.

They tumble turn
At our feet like swimmers,
And clatter in panic
Back up the lane.
Wild midnight badgers!

Alan Brown

Akol and the Giraffe

In the burning African sun a great famine came to the Sudan

In the burning African sun,
locusts ate the grain;
people, cattle, goats and chickens died.
Buffalo, antelope, lion, elephant and bird
migrated to far away rivers.

In the burning African sun,
seven brothers waited in a cattle shed to die –
until Akol, the eldest – feeling his responsibility –
dragged himself out to hunt.
He hadn't gone far when exhaustion overcame him;
he stumbled and fell asleep…
in the burning African sun.

A tall, elegant giraffe and her calf
happened upon him;
they breathed cool breath upon his face, allowing him life.
Akol awoke
and tried again to walk,
desperate for his brothers to know he had not abandoned them.
In silent grace the giraffes
followed him,
made a shade for him to walk in,
tendered their tails for him to hang on to.
Akol was filled with the knowledge that God and the spirit of his ancestors,
working through the giraffes, had saved his life that day…
in the burning African sun.

Akol's brothers glimpsed the group approaching and,
hungry for meat,
took up their spears
for the kill.

In the burning African sun,
Akol Adiangbar cried,
'From this day on
all giraffes will become members of our clan – they will
never again be hunted in our land.
We shall become the Padiangbar clan
– the house of gentle, lean and tall people.'

In that moment, clouds gathered;
rain fell.
Akol felt the drops upon his face
and cried tears of relief,
knowing his brothers were saved.

And that is how the giraffe
became the sacred animal of the
Padiangbar people
– the gentle, lean and tall people
of Southern Sudan
in the burning African sun.

All proceeds from this poem go to the mission to create Schools Under the Trees, for those Sudanese children whose schools have been stolen from them by war.

Adapted from legend by Irene Yates

How the Tortoise Got its Shell

Come to my feast!
cried the great god Zeus.
Today I shall be wed!
And from each corner of the earth
all Zeus's creatures sped ...

The fliers and the creepers,
the long, the short, the tall;
the crawlers and the leapers,
the feathered, furred and bald;
hunters, biters, finders, fighters,
hooters, whistlers, roarers;
squeakers, screamers, squawkers, dreamers,
nibblers, gulpers, borers.
Paws and claws from hills and shores
from south, from north, from west and east,
from mountain tops and forest floors
all Zeus's creatures joined the feast
except
the tortoise.

They raved, they pranced, they feasted, danced;
six days and nights each creature stayed
to chatter, flatter, clap and cheer
at the great god Zeus's grand parade
except
the tortoise.

Next day ...
Why weren't you there, my friend, asked Zeus,
the day that I was wed?

The tortoise smiled her small, slow smile
and raised her small, slow head.

A wedding feast is fun, I guess,
but I'm a simple one.
I'm happy by myself, she said.
There's no place quite like home!

How dare you stay away! roared Zeus.
I'll show you just what for!
From this day on you'll carry your home
on your back, for evermore!

Judith Nicholls

Hurt No Living Thing

Hurt no living thing;
Ladybird, nor butterfly,
Nor moth with dusty wing,
Nor cricket chirping cheerily,
Nor grasshopper so light of leap,
Nor dancing gnat, nor beetle fat,
Nor harmless worms that creep.

Christina Rossetti

Insect

I nvertebrate

N ifty

S ix-legged

E arth-invading

C reepy-crawly

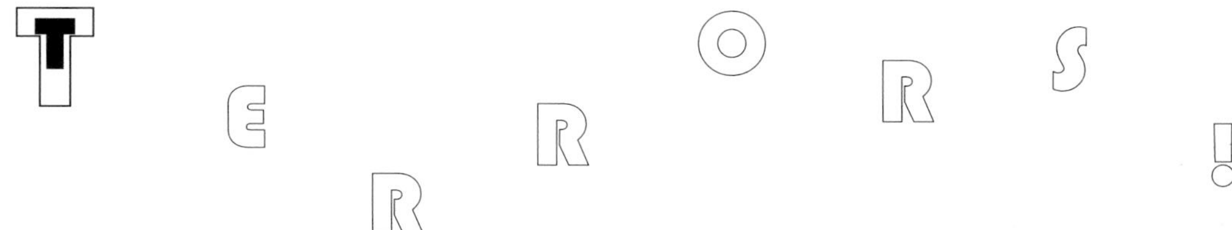

Judith Nicholls

Advice about Dogs

A dog knocks once at everybody's door.

A dog on the swings
is worth two on the roundabouts.

You can't teach an old dog to butter parsnips.

Great Danes from little acorns grow.

You can give a dog fine feathers
but he won't lay golden eggs.

Every dog has a silver lining.

Don't put all your dogs in one basket.

Let sleeping dogs count the chickens.

Irene Rawnsley

Jabberwocky

'Twas brillig, and the slithy toves
Did gyre and gimble in the wabe:
All mimsy were the borogoves,
And the mome raths outgrabe.

'Beware the Jabberwock, my son!
The jaws that bite, the claws that catch!
Beware the Jubjub bird, and shun
The frumious Bandersnatch!'

He took his vorpal sword in hand:
Long time the manxome foe he sought –
So rested he by the Tumtum tree,
And stood awhile in thought.

And, as in uffish thought he stood,
The Jabberwock, with eyes of flame,
Came whiffling through the tulgey wood,
And burbled as it came!

One, two! One, two! And through and through
The vorpal blade went snicker-snack!
He left it dead, and with its head
He went galumphing back.

'And hast thou slain the Jabberwock?
Come to my arms, my beamish boy!
O frabjous day! Callooh! Callay!'
He chortled in his joy.

'Twas brillig, and the slithy toves
Did gyre and gimble in the wabe:
All mimsy were the borogoves,
And the mome raths outgrabe.

Lewis Carroll

Death

Fat, squashed toad,
poisoned rat,
dewed rabbit,
mouse mown flat.
Hedgehog bleeds –
fleas retire.
Velvet-black mole attire shredded by sharp, owl claws–
what use pink, paddle paws? Feathers fly glued to earth.
Waxed and warm worms of death wriggle from black cat's zip.
Backstroke bee's
final dip. Sticky
snail's caravan,
cracked, caved in.
Beetles ran - - -
under shoes,
nowit r a i n s
washing death
down the drains.

Gina Douthwaite

Births

WEBFOOT

To Drip (nee Mudwet) and Flapper, at Duckend Maternity Nest On April 1st, twin eggs. Both cracked.

Marriages

WEBFOOT - WADDLE

Mr. and Mrs. F. Webfoot, of Lakeside, wish to announce the marriage of their twin daughter Puddle, to Shaky, 10th son of Mr. and Mrs. Q. Waddle of Waterstown. The wedding will take place at Ditchbottom Chapel, at dawn on Saturday, followed by a reception at the Stagnant Pond Hotel.

Deaths

WADDLE

Puddle, dear wife of Shaky. By accident. The funeral will be held on Squashy Corner, at rush hour. Donations please, in aid of Duck Safety, to the lollipop lady. *Rest in Reeds.*

Gina Douthwaite

Lambs

On legs ten sizes too big
newly knit lambs
head-butt the pole
that grows from their hillside.
In a lamb gang they practise
being rams

then spring, like jacks-from-boxes,
and scatter in a clockwork dash
to head-butt a milky mum.

Gina Douthwaite

Nick's Cat

Slick cat,

quick cat,

flick a bit o' stick cat,

chase a ghost of rat cat,

make a nest of mat cat,

curl up in a hat cat,

lick a coat that's thick cat –

sick cat.

Nick's cat.

Gina Douthwaite

Seagulls in the City

Chaos in the playground at tuck time ...
Two hundred and fifty crisp-eaters
Jostle for space.
Drinks and biscuits
Apple cores
Chocolate bars
Nuts and raisins
Bits of sandwich
Monster crunchies
Jelly frogs -
Everybody munches,
Squabbles over
Delicious titbits,
Discards unwanted crumb.

The bell goes and we all stand to attention,
Tuck consumed,
Bellies comfortingly full,
And wait to be sent in.

At dead on quarter to eleven,
Every single morning,
A swoop of seagulls drops down from nowhere.
Like some huge white blizzard spilling out of the sky
A screeching, scrawking,
Squealing, stealing chorus
Takes over our playground,
Battles for the rich pickings of our junk food crumbs.

The Silent Snake

The birds go fluttering in the air,
The rabbits run and skip,
Brown squirrels race along the bough,
The May-flies rise and dip;
But, whilst these creatures play and leap,
The silent snake goes creepy-creep!

The birds a-sing and whistle loud,
The busy insects hum,
The squirrels chat, the frogs say 'Croak!'
But the snake is always dumb.
With not a sound through grasses deep
The silent snake goes creepy-creep!

Anonymous

Author Index

Title Index